c o n j u r e
blues

Jaki Shelton Green

poems

conjure
blues

Carolina Wren Press   Durham, North Carolina

Several of the poems in this book were first published in The African-American Review and Women's Words, A Journal of Carolina Writing.

"Conjure Blues" was published in a different form (as "Untitled") in Black Poetry of the '80s from the Deep South: Word Up (Beans & Brown Rice, Atlanta, GA).

This publication is supported by a grant from the North Carolina Arts Council and was made possible in part through gifts to the Durham Arts Council United Arts Fund and support from the city of Durham.

Acknowledgments
Special thanks to David Kellogg for being such a supportive editor. To my mother, brother, and children for smoothing my edges, to all my family and friends for keeping me honest, and to my wonderful sister-in-law Sharon: the reader and "keeper" of the manuscripts . . .

Front cover photograph copyright © 1996 by Roger Manley
Author photograph by Jan G. Hensley

Library of Congress Cataloging-in-Publication Data
Conjure blues: poems/ Jaki Shelton Green. —1st ed. p. cm.
ISBN 0-932112-37-4
1. Afro-American families—Poetry. 2. Afro-American women—
Poetry. 3. Afro-Americans—Poetry. I. Title.
PS3557.R3723C6 1996
811'.54—dc20

Project editor: David Kellogg

Copyedited by A. H. Selch

Designed by Meredith Brickell
and Heather Hensley of 6 foot studio

Carolina Wren Press
120 Morris Street
Durham, NC 27701

To the memory of

my beloved Grandmother

and Father.

table of contents

conjure
blues₁

conjure

gathering rain

i am a vessel
porous
waiting for your downpour
waiting for your
rain
to drench
swell within me

i am a basket
woven
intertwined
knotted
rewoven
waiting to be
filled
emptied
refilled

i am a cup
round

deep
oval
circular
waiting to be
filled
emptied
refilled
waiting to be
held
cupped

drink.

i am a box
flat
round
square
triangular
waiting to be
closed
hidden
filled
locked

i am your mystery
find me
close me
open me
await my
pouring
my opening
my closing

i am a woman
waiting.

imani

the first time your tiny lips searched for
my breast i knew that your soul had
decided to stay
grandma taught me babies were
spirits whispers wind souls cruising
through time sometimes they stayed
sometimes they roamed back into the
womb wanting/needing to come again
knowing their birthing time
the first time i smelled you i knew
the earth flowers would be jealous
would feel diminished by your smell of
wind   ocean   sky
your taste was the taste of seed and
clouds and rain
your screams were the last thunderbolts
of my grandmother's woman tribe
we buried your veil beneath the
sage peppermint and blood root.
i knew you would stay

you first dreamed of horses with no
heads who stood at your bed
laughing at you
their heads somewhere else
riding the night
you would talk to the moon
inside your crib
choreograph oriental operas
your tongue tasting herstory through woven quilts
of grandmothers past and grandmothers here
your cheeks sleeping on the
stitches of fear   tiredness
happy stitches
strong stitches
patterned stitches of yourself
telling a life ready to happen.

eva/jaki/ivory/imani/eva

in the season of rising up in the morning
granddaughter give new meaning
to great day in the sky
sky with small
fists, pinching clouds
reshaping stars
into skirts
wearing moon shadows like capes
we turn raindrops into buttons
stitch hair balls along the hems of
dresses
fire dresses
new granddaughters
wear new earth clothes
spell their name sistuh
prepare new warriors
to prepare new earths
check skirts for hems lined with hail dust
never admitting to treason

visions

for richard

we come into this world
like brides in ivory veils
life lifts them one by one
until the whole face
opens the world and beckons
and we follow like
the nile fishermen
following morning rain
we follow like the
ones before us
followed
the ones with cracked
palms
following
reaching
like the stillborn
ghost of a child with new eyes
we follow like the mothers

of sculptors follow
armless
caught in a storm
of birth

we come into this world like
brides in ivory veils
love lifts them one by one
until the whole face
laughs
cries
we pray to this face god
screaming into
copper earth
listen to clouds
whisper to veiled mornings
we who call ourselves women
rise
walk
iron hips beat out rhythms
sweat beside proud chests
sway
this natural rhythm of love
unaware of stares
these selves called women
walk directly into this
map called man

we come into this world like
brides in ivory veils
we wait for the storm
to lift this veil
we come like death horses
carrying our lives' story neatly
folded/starched

like fine linen
in large wicker urns
only this life
is easily scorched
this life of love does not
fold easily
is too large for
wicker baskets

we fold our fears
put them away
now standing
touching with our eyes
with smiles
our day is today
soft and delicious
a day that is so easy
to open and be a part of

a day full of mouths
always kissing
and arms and legs that
dance with the wind
we have paled the sun today
our thoughts are radiant
as we untie knots
and retie knots that touch
us—we are the golden
instrument that begs to be
played. listen
to our symphonies.

eva

numbers are a dance i danced
in the secret place
herbs are the jewels we
lost during the passage
new tongues burn unleavened bread
tongues spoken from the ears
are seen at night
and only precede midnight rainbows
we played the games of
the rabbits
you taught me how to listen to the
quarrels between mr and mrs tree spirit
and walk invisible through the meadow
thank you for the secrets between
white bread and magical nothingness
tasting like the first fruit
ah teacher of rhythm
and practice
and belief in demons of the light

who steal her soul in kodak wonder
thank you for muscadine hunts
thank you for the secrets
of strawberry and blackberry dew
and the difference between linen
and taffeta
easter and christmas
there are secrets tucked away inside
dresser drawers breathing quietly
your secrets line my dresser/my closets
rhinestones feathers lace buttons
polka dot scarves patent leather
cashmere lambswool chenille
i found a piece of camphor beside my
pillow this morning
you the clever one who prayed
nightly who searched the woods of
your dreams searching for
womb roots to make more
secrets breathe

i know the grandmother one had hands

i know the grandmother one had hands
but they were always in bowls
folding, pinching, rolling the dough
making the bread
i know the grandmother one had hands
but they were always under water
sifting rice
blueing clothes
starching lives
i know the grandmother one had hands
but they were always in the earth
planting seeds
removing weeds
growing knives
burying sons
i know the grandmother one had hands
but they were always under
the cloth

pushing it along
helping it birth into
a skirt
a dress
curtains to lock out the
night
i know the grandmother one had hands
but they were always inside
the hair
parting
plaiting
twisting it into rainbows
i know the grandmother one had hands
but they were always inside
pockets
holding the knots
counting the twisted veins
holding onto herself
lest her hands disappear
into sky
i know the grandmother one had hands
but they were always inside the clouds
poking holes for the
rain to fall.

the lesson

your earrings
your brooches
your shawls
your bible all whisper:
    tell my story
    tell my story
    you granddaughter one
    it is your name
    daughter-grand-grand little one
    it means to tell . . .
    tell my story.

you cannot know the story your daughters will whisper
until you tell my story . . .
you can not find the words of *yourself*
to give to your daughter
until you tell my story. this story.
the earrings fall from my ears
the brooch no longer fastens

the shawl grows holes that laugh—
the wind opens the bible to the
proverbs of your life
i listen
i write
i collect herbs and bathe in them as you
instruct me
i ride the wind wearing the blue and white of your eyes
i wait. when i was ten you chased hens around the
back yard—snapped their necks, burned your headrag
stitched quilts that were meant for
cold New England mornings.

showed me how to make fire with my
hands wide open

showed me how to shave butterflies
so their wings would fan
wider
so my poems could
fly with them
from bush to bush
telling your story.

eclipses of eva

another mr john, mr otis, or mr tom
had died
i was six, first grade
smocked pink dresses from aunt cordelia
your big hand wrapped my small one
tight. gloved. like snow on sand
grandma why we coming to funerals?
that what good folks do
why they keep dying?
that's what you come here to do.
you tucked my plaits inside the collar
of the blue velvet coat
with matching hat
i hated this coat
you hated it too
but you agreed with mama that it was so
upper-class correct
that's what you wanted too
for me to always act like who we were

free black people
with free minds

but the blue velvet coat was everything
but free
a twelve-button prison without windows
without pockets waiting to be poked full of holes

aunt cordelia made me pretty dresses
plaids, corduroy, taffeta, dotted swiss
mama would brush my hair
and brush my hair
but curls would not leave.
you preferred braids.
you'd let me brush your hair
part it
grease it
plait it into one large basket
then we'd play "mommy"
you said your mama was always away
being a mommy to white children
when you were little
so i had to be the mommy
for you
that's when i liked you the most
i was a good mommy
i'd let you draw pictures
teach you to sew like you taught me
you always drew better pictures than mine
maybe you'd been practicing all those years
back when your mama was being a mommy
somewhere for someone else.

thunderstorms were best of all
you'd pull a chair

right up to the window and talk to God
for a long time
you'd be talking a mile a minute
real low, every once in a while i'd pick up a
word. nothing more
you could talk to the Lord better than anybody
i'd ever known
he seemed to be talking back whenever you'd laugh,
closing your eyes, talking in hushed screams
then you'd sit and just rock
back and forth
back and forth
with your eyes closed
more words
racing like a train . . .
you prayed long prayers at night too
i never thought the Lord would hear you
in your teeny weeny whispering night voice
your prayer voice you called it
but i know better now

you eva tate's grandgirl ain't cha?
no, i'm mrs eva tate's granddaughter
you the one she used to take wit her
everywhere she went? how she doing?
my grandmother is fine. real fine. thank you.

cleansing skies

for my wombpeople

I

    in circles of red we swam
    drinking until our mouths
    full of gravity, full of sky
    lifted our halos above the nets
    of dried womanness

II

    parting scalps with
    the lavender of witch-blades
    we created
    new heads

III

faces born behind
veiled glass
break into crepe de chine dresses
red fox stockings
filene's bargain pillboxes
ermine-lined mouths

IV

in circles of red
we sucked the skin from her bones
we drank
the placenta's froth

V

oshun will choose the fire
for the circle
i choose the stones.
bring me the silver cup
to hold obatala's bracelets

VI

it is this sister thing
stalking you
inviting you outside
choose your own weapon

VII

bring me flowers
from the eggplant
nine eggs from
three pregnant doves

VIII

male chickens will not do

IX

in the circle of white
breathe deeply
bathe alone
you must scream
to break the aura
of shadows

X

you sister
you sweet mama
you sweet stuff
you miss girl
you miss fly girl
you sister thang
woman thang
you who be such a
whole woman but you
be bad bad still
gitting badder thang
you who own all the corners
and all the crossroads
i will do your bidding

XI

fill your hallowed vulva
with honey.
drink silently.

XII

when the bracelets
of crystal and white beads meet
soon
the strings of his heart will pop
a father
a brother
a lover
who hurts
remind him
your color
is white
it will swallow his
swords
as easily as the
fire eater swallows
red

XIII

wait for a new path
inside the face

XIV

wait for a bronze song
from the east

XV

wait for a new bracelet
when crystal beads
meet white beads
the strings of his heart
draw tight
form knots
pray to be unraveled

XVI

the child gave birth
to several faces
we chose
woman
we chose
blood

XVII

you girl
girl friend
friend girl
friday girl
miss lady
sunday girl
you who be trying out
this woman thang
can i buy one
of your bracelets
can i sit on your corner

XVIII

big girl poems, stories, curses
litanies, divinations
popping out of too tight lips,
waterjaws, cryface
when y'all git pissed
y'all be wailing
can i buy a piece of your
world
can i get a bid
on this new moon
can i spread my
velvetness across your

bruised soul
can i get inside
your corner
of sistuh stuff

XIX

big girl poems
will get your ass
in trouble

conjure
blues2

conjure blues

are you sure you want to travel this
red rope hair
blood locks
dripping history like a faucet
without gaskets
are you sure you want to travel
this path of kinky trails
interlaced with the breath of
ghanaian ghosts
this rope hair coarse this
rope hair full of tears this red
rope hair braiding little
splintered brains in Alabama
binding arms back to torsos
in Johannesburg
this rope hair wrapping
knives inside of babys' blankets
planting bullets under sunflower
beds

rope hair red rope hair
which wraps and unwraps your
nighttime fears your
white years of guilt
your nighttime tastes
of black lace, black woman
love
black braids unwrapping
unleashing unforgiving
red rope hair
are you sure you want to
travel this road
point to this cloud
wish upon this star
swinging from red rope hair
a lynching or a suicide
red rope hair strangling your truths
  my legacy our pain
  choking our offspring
  red rope hair a road
  crawl only no running
now i lay you
  down to sleep
  red rope hair stealing you at
  sunrise a sun crucifix a sun
  snake racing falling sleeping
  blood rope

prayer for jessie

I

i will smear blood under your eyes
stand in the same dream with you
hear your secret screams
i will watch the light pump your heart
and worship whatever dream that swallows you
your silence will not protect you
for i have declared war
your speaking will cease
will be stopped
you will fear the visibility of my children's eyes
without which you cannot really live
we have declared a funny wartime
i stopped by your doorstep
stole your footprints
followed your shadow dropping
3 grains of sand from each print
i placed your footprints in the small
bags woven by African grandmothers

i will carry your footprints with me for 3 days
you and i will meet at the crossroads
i will toss your footprints in the direction
i want you to go
children play a funny kinda war

II

grandma used to say your mama
and your mama's mama didn't know nothing
about babies born with veils
for surely you were born with a veil
a veil that they did not bury properly in the
proper place at the proper time
grandma said you were such an evil white
boy because you'd seen the face of your own
devil
said if they'd buried that veil you woulda been
marching right up there on tv with dr king
instead of spitting on colored folks every night
after the news
grandma and miss gaynell said that the midwife
who delivered you musta put a curse on you
just because you chose to
come her way on that day

III

in your grandfather's barn
they found 12 white wax candles
    a bag of oranges
    several raw eggs
    a bloody towel
    2 ducks
    4 wingless pigeons
    7 fish
    a baby goat
they found all this spread on top of a bed
of chopped apples and oranges
facing east was a drawing of you
only your arms were birdlike
your hair dreadlocked
your skin like ash

IV

grandma said they shoulda buried that veil
but then white folks don't know no better
if i were you i'd find me some scorpion heads,
9 needles and bake 'em in a cake
if i were you i'd dig in the earth and
claim me a veil
if i were you grandma said you should go
to the altar grind you up some
high john the conqueror and pray for rain

v

when i was a little girl all the grown folks around
me watched you every night
talked about you must be somebody's
necessary evil
you musta been somebody's mojo that had gone bad
these same old folks later sat on porches
rocked in the dark
hummed your name
stitching the sounds in the darkness with forked
needles
and even now from my grandmother's grave
she watches over you
saying lawd chile god show don't like ugly
she's singing sometimes
saying chile you oughta go to the altar
you oughta light you a broomstraw
you oughta find out where your mama hid
that first lock of hair she cut from your
baby scalp
grandma said you oughta go to the altar
oughta sprinkle some cast off evil incense
on the floormat of your car
grandma said you better read the 27th psalm
for 9 mornings in a row
yeah
you need to come by here
and listen to the slaves crying
and dance in their lynching light
you need to come by here and ask
for mercy

VI

　　your silence will not protect you for
　　we are a warring people
　　known for capturing truth
　　known to stop sentences in midair
　　your speaking will cease
　　you will fear the eyes of all children
　　you ought to get to the altar
　　and speak in tongues

tribute to the men and women who perished in the Imperial Chicken Plant fire in Hamlet, North Carolina

(a conversation i overheard in the fire)

there is still a sadness stuck in my mouth
that makes me wanna suck
on something that i have not tasted
for so long
what does it mean to not be able to remember
your mama's breast
bronze nipples, rising, falling,
but the blues remember
so without being able to explain
i feel this song surging inside of me
grinning, shouting
i feel this song my every question,
my why for, my how come,
my what did i do to be so black and blue
and it answers me by and by

in this new grave i choose
it answers like a moan.
no train came through those doors
no train whistle took us
out of there   no train crossing
red waters
no more welfare blues
no more politician blues
this morning has come
even down here
i got the same human hunger blues
and the blues hugged me back
as i watched my own hands
leave their prints on the fire's tongue
the blues hugged me back
when i closed eyes for the last time
and counted
mandingo
fulani
ashanti
ibo
counted all of us
before the fiery lynch rope
wrapped its tongue
around our throats.
the blues.
what else could i wail
what else would carry me
across yonder field of fire
not even the black of the bruise
could be called anything but red
i got the red fire blues
whatever we were as chicken workers,
never mind, whatever they tried to make us be,

no matter
our humanity
sang survival
we were white but the fire begat black
we were black and the fire begat black
together,
we became blue
blues people
and the blues bespoke our souls
in the church
my children sang strange words
to flat rhythms
they could not climb or ride on
king jesus was on the other side of Hamlet
maybe he was checking birth certificates
driver's licenses, taxes
but he didn't bring no train
to bust through the door
i carry my past deep
inside these earth pockets
as my children sing flat notes
do they make love in heaven
are there brass beds
any music for people to party by
i guess it would take a blues man
to track me down up here
a blue black blues man
but not black like shackled nights or cotton
row black, or welfare line black
but JAZZ BLACK
blues black
soft black
any kind of song
can make a slave strong

but it's the BLUES SONG
describing to my baby
how my feet burned first
how my hands were broken in 38 places
how my hair became the sun
omega and alpha brilliant
a new shade of red
any kind of song
can make a slave strong
but it's the BLUES SONG
describing to my mama
that i tried to recall
the contours of her breast
the bronze nipple

the coming of changó

late last night she remembers everyone
but feels no one. no. thing
to remember who she might be
who her husband might be
only shadows
only faces
just one of the faces she's borne in time
it's time again to sleep
she feels her dying face
and watches shadows of other lost faces
play upon her ceilings
she knows the time is ripe
she knows that the heirloom dresser
lined with snuff, folded faded memories
and keepsakes from mother's days past
has eyes that watch her gasping
for breath
that watch the skin stretch
and swell

the chair behind the door holds quilts
sewn with pleasant meditation
the chair watches also with
shameful curiosity
as this body of woman
rises in constant agony
trying to stretch into the quilt and become a
square of patchwork
she winks first at the chair
then the dresser and touches
the lump inside her gown
this lump of herstory tied/knotted
in a handkerchief
that great-grandchildren
gifted to her on some other ancient
forgotten occasion
a mother a grandmother a great-
grandmother
her vision has splintered spaces
for her offspring
untamed
singing field songs
her vision knows quiet
that means danger
knows herbal wonders
knows a caravan of exotic wanderers
here in this bed that has become
the sea here in her quiet ocean
private voices whispering voices
speak through her veins
speak through her stained gown
speak of whole flesh
beneath this fever
she realizes time is only an edge moving into new

rivers
beneath this fever
and red cheeks
and fire tongue
beneath the years
that hold that fear of an edge
that edge she remembers
when as a young girl
she waded in mud
in cotton fields potato fields
any field
where the sky
hung low
where thunder bent down
and ran through her hips
thighs her swelling belly
the edge where she
squatted with fear giving
birth to sons beside rivers
washing knives to cut
this umbilicus from God
under a half moon
half sun   in campfires
where fires were silver like
nightfall
her head drifts and she feels
butterflies whistling in her ears
windtunes
suddenly she fears stars
blinking at noontime
she hears petals breaking outside
her grandchildren try to hold
back the sky
but are crushed by this edge

that cracks open her house and
enters her bed
this edge
red and big
and crystal clear
young white healthy clean hands
enter her room
she sings a song
knowing they will strip the robe
begin her burial
strong healthy white hands
with knives
dark words
white teeth
hold the dark palm
she recalls squatting before
with thighs high wide
spitting out child pellets
wounding only the myths of time
now thighs remain stone as she watches
her burial unfold
in this metallic
clean
white
health place
she watches them remove
her intestines
she waits as they remove
ribs and place them
beneath her bosoms
like newborns are placed
but this rib stillborn
does not cry and shudder
limbs come next and are placed

beside her cheeks
no gentleness
but rock sharp curves
in the dying time
her grandchildren dance
their children howl and moan
their dark songs
pierce her womb
and flare her nostrils
a dying time
a dying time
sunbleached breasts
rise and fall
scream and dance away
we all notice the marks
above her children's eyes
crystalline crosses magic voodoo
reminding us of the great high
sunsets
reminding us of calvary
other crosses.

ode to lies

i am tired of the earth
it is too heavy
has too many edges
not enough moments
it is too narrow
for passage of this pain
i am tired of the truth
it holds too many bridles
too many whips
too many prisons
lie to me   set me free
make me dance   bleed   scream
pray for the shower of lies
to drown this canyon

insult

bacon is burning again
overdue notices form a multicolored border
around the dresser mirror
his back is long, firm
rich redbrown like the glistening
tables he makes with his bare hands
it is a good back
bacon is smoking the kitchen
why does he not cook it in the oven
breakfast is in the yellow bedroom
he peels eggshells too hot boiled
she sits elbows at attention
sucking on mandarin orange slices
champagne boiled eggs oranges melba
he talks about the new woods from
brazil while the weatherman
comics the thunderstorms gaining
momentum in the south
it is a yellow bedroom

the egg yolk is running
splashes on his thigh
she wants to start there
licking the spill from his
hardness
only he'd push her aside and never understand
that she doesn't want to fuck
just enjoy breakfast

things break down

things break down in different ways
like love
it's been ten years since
i've been thin
things break down in different ways
like the absence of his smile
things break down in different ways
like the meadows of the skin
apples spoil
meat rots
aspirin takes care of toothache but
things break down in different ways
like the last time he praised my art
stood in my mirror
things break down in different ways
like sunday morning blues
getting sung out at the altar
i said things break down
in different ways

like my clock stopping
one morning at 3 a.m.
he crashed his car into the river
things break down
      his toothbrush is still
beside the mirror

the crucian tracks

I

the rivers spilled
crooked fish
into open mouths

> *aqoliagbo*
> *aqoliagbo*

do not come near

white gloves
hold back
black rivers

> dance with me
> dance with me

the river gods
removed their faces
dance the river dance
crooked fish swam backwards

II

(on watching the sunset)

you stole mud from the basins of Iowa autumn
to reshape your face
conceal the face
reveal the summer's massacre of
broken instruments
weeping poems
shadowless dances
the mud became your plaster for walls
of a house
doorless
windowless
you slept hard under caribbean night
i slept alone.
in Frederikstead there is the music
of horses on the beach
rasta men with chests larger than their dreams
enchant their hoofs
ride the horses with passion
i click aimless kodak.
the horse is another devil

III

in my house the geckos do not gather
they come one by one
peer at the eyeless horses guarding my bed.

conjure

blues 3

this slave woman voice continues to emerge

continues to seep into the mindset

bids me to write about wombs with teeth

wombs holding poison for penises erect with racism

erect with sexism   bids me to write

about wombs that swallow white men

wombs   directs me to write about

the death at orgasm   the orgasm of death

yes sisters   i will do your bidding

apartheid

on the blackest continent
there is an indigo tide
that i ride
not caring whose skeletons
danced here before
not caring what black skeletons
will reveal to this princess child
to this lovely creature
on the blackest continent
the sky is bluer wider and higher
more open to to black daughters singing
nearer my god to thee

in the blackness of this continent
the sun is anxious to shine on her children
anxious to hear the prayers of
Soweto Pretoria Selma Virginia Beach
on this blackest island
the sky opened up
through a window i saw

the words disguised as
clouds and the clouds
screamed lonely no more
lonely no more
nearer my god to thee
lonely no more

auction block

open your legs gal
ain't gonna tell you no mo
now step right up you fine
virginia men of class
step right up and look at this here
gal's hole
now that's a well for a lot of drinking

aunt sue spread her legs wide
as six white men stepped forward to bid
on this hole
a hole that will soon suck them up into
its darkness
a darkness as wide as deep as her geography

aunt sue was bought by master peterson who
had a twitch for large African wenches
master peterson would visit aunt sue each
3rd full moon wednesday
she now knew how to predict his restlessness

her children by him continued to look
negroid
as if her body knew its own being
and refused to acknowledge his white seed
these children grew
disappearing before their mother's eyes
disappeared as a wedding present
to master peterson's sister down in
south carolina
disappeared when master peterson got drunk
in georgia and lost three slave boys
to a gambler
disappeared in exchange for a new set of
mules to the horse breeder in kentucky
third wednesdays
full moons
aunt sue gathered nettleweed
saved strands of third wednesday hair
gathered blood from miz peterson's "monthly"
stitched out psalms using master peterson's hair
stood bone naked against the elm tree
of her father's lynching in midnight sounds
her womb gathering teeth from the rain

aura cleansing

they came in African adornment
they came in silenced splendor, raw as
honey, brickcolors
fuchsia
violet
but always black
they came crowned
they came plaited   unplaited
but they came
strutting   humming   whispering
carrying ribbons
ribbons reaching around a world
ribbons tied in front of young sisters
ribbons tied behind wiser sisters
but each tying ribbons to each other
in this time some died
some were born
some were buried

some unburied
but we came
discovering
only to be discovered

skin mirror

where does the slave woman face
find reflection
the mirrors of broken-winged birds
the eyes of children in flight
the wide-open death panes of lost
crystals full of age full of blood

where does the slave woman
see herself
know her smile
check the creases of lips
know her own bone structure
know her own beauty
know her hair texture
know the secrets of her neckline. know the swell in her nipples
it was in the skin's eye of
bloodroot sisters
new sister children
created
wide mirrors of face

unraveling

you remember things about me that i have remembered
to forget
but then there are no longer "first moments"
nothing unrehearsed any longer
no risk of meeting a soul unclothed and yet
you bear the bleeding holes inside your chest
i count them with my lips'
circling balm of gilead
into the fire pits
i was not prepared for
your undressed face
i wanted a mask
an excuse to wear
my most recently constructed mask armored
with coiling veils
known to strangle upon touch
yes i wanted your face painted
in reds, purples, blues, anything
but the sun, the rain, the child's secret
i sat counting the holes looking for

strong surface within your chest
where i could stand firmly
and raise my hands to stitch and weave
new circles inside crusting wounds
circles that have magic
circles that see in the dark
circles that pray the prayer
of tongues
new circles
beginning to re-create a name
you can wear when you go away
if there were mountains
we would have jumped into the valley of names
no hills between us
only smooth polished earth bordered by sun and moon
becoming the darkest white moment
for you
the most white darkness
for me.
we relearn to breathe and
say good-bye.

this eggó is alive

"never go to the woods alone"

I

her bosom was full of scars for she had
crawled many miles, face down, drinking
dew from grass, swallowing earth.
she arrived at my door bloody with the
scent of birth and death clenched in her
mouth. she told me stories of old women
bearing children alone, burying them inside
the warmth of leaves and feathers, and
butterfly scarves. she told me more than
once to love from the inside out, the
same way at five she taught me to put
my coat on from the inside out
flip it over my head arms straight.
"i was too old to rest my head in your lap
when you returned" i said to her one day
alone, beside her grave.
but then you were too young when you

returned to me. i became the nurturing
one. you the child. i applied ointment
to your scars. you drank of my wisdom.
your stories for my children were too
old, too fragile, too alone as stories
to hold up to the light. we listened
hard. waited for your endings
waited for your beginnings

II

i remember learning to drink water out of dippers
cool well water. nine year olds running onto some neighbor's
back porch for a drink.
parched lips enjoying the taste of water and
aluminum on those hot days
you would take me with you and miss mary to the meadow
i was full of joy and fright
the meadow was a magical place. i never understood then why we went
to the meadow. now i understand womenlore, i can count my years
now with the measuring of bloodroot and simmering sassafras.
now i know the secret smells of queens who hunt for the jewels
of the earth. the ground contains jewels brighter than the sun
the ground in all its darkness contains the star. the star of
life. the star inside the womb that serves as a floodlight to
new life in search of mothers. so the meadow and the mystery of
wells would stay in my mind for many years growing up. the
knowledge of wells became easily accessible for me, i now understand
the engineering, the process, the earth's underground. but the
meadow remains a mystery many times since you left, i've gone
back into the woods. walked the same direction, same distance
no meadow. no magical forest. as if you folded it away with you

praise song

you woman tree woman one
swaying to unheard of winds uninvented air streams
you woman sky with palms broad enough to hold egypt
who taught me to walk
slow and deliberate
like i had somewhere to go
who taught me stories
that needed telling
to love men and women who needed
who taught me to fetch life
out of the depths of rivers
taught me the words
that the tree branches sang to wake
the sun and bring morning home
who taught me to love loving
with my eyes wide open
who taught me to dance and smile
in rhythm
to clap with an open heart

imani

i watch your smile travel to the
four corners of your woman face
it gathers nerve
a new momentum
as it signals newness
womanness
i have not known your face as woman
my first born
my first one
my new self
i am learning to speak in whole sentences
learning not to speak always
in the mother tongue
we are learning that we can be sisters
that we can open the curtains together
that we can each call morning
something else

harvest song

I

eyes moist from the morning
it is teeth we should grow
you said
i listened to your hoe
striking the dust

II

mothers sing toothless lullabies
hold blankets full of wormholes
swallow breath

III

in the windowless church
the daughters of deuteronomy
sons of joshua, john, and luke
puke on the sacrament
make new wine
slash new wrists

IV

    the teeth grow without water
    without sunlight
    need no weeding

V

    i harvest you during ramadan
    and the season of grandfathers

VI

    the dancers gather with the poets
    who sleep beside musicians potters
    sculptors mask makers

VII

    and what shall we feast on
    with new teeth

conjure
blues4

conjure

the griot's song

this man on the edge of the sun
speaking with truth-laced tongues
calls my name
he is the one who met me
in the dust storm
i was riding on the wind
into the mountains when i
heard his shadow
scream
suddenly canyons grew out of rivers
and the sunlight
    became a throb
    a drum beat
the veins in his heart
    dusty but full of fire
gave shadow to the new sun

tidal surge

the laying on of hands
at daybreak
eclipsed by the laugh
in your smile
interrupted by wind
interrupted by sand
your eyes bear witness
to the arrival
of morning
i smile back
through the eyes of this
new storm
this new singing cloud
this new rain
i smile back
through the eye borrowed
from our first storm
we hold back other nights

you present
the laying on
of hands
crystals
that bend
into the
shape of your
eyes
that see
through the
curtains
that lift
new veils
other brides
other samenesses
we smile
at ourselves
salvaged

acquaint ourselves
over the sameness
embarrassed by the need
to need
the need to be

dry inside
the storm

i cry

it is my father's ashes glistening
on barren branches
the clouds were bloodstained
in the shadows
of ritual
called crossing
to name is to replace
to praise is to erase
to dance is to fall.
blood stains on red skin
need not be removed
from the lips of
children unnamed
or from the red crosses
in skies untouched
to touch is to smear
martin's voice was a piano key
this morning
out of tune

sharp
it is my father's ashes glistening
on barren branches
blood falling on earth
fertilizing the good
earth
dance martin
claim your own
cloud

that boy from georgia
is coming through here

they changed curtains
waxed floors
aired out the front company room
sent for camphor to lay throughout the house
they cooked all night
boiled bath water all day
cornbread, okra, turnip salad, stewed chicken,
fried chicken, dressing,
killed the prized hen
gravy, corn, potatoes, rice, sweet potato custard,
lemon pie, rice pudding, coconut cake,
chocolate cake, lemonade, and your chittluns,
martin,
all for you martin.
word was given Sunday
that you was coming
to their corner
so they swept dirt yards

put the chickens up
hung out the special quilt
laid out the catalog sheets
put fresh oil in all the lamps
cause you never could tell
just how long you'd want to stay
a war on evil takes a lot of planning
takes a lot to get troops
stirred up.
so stewed corn with fatback, fried chicken
sliced tomatoes and cucumbers in vinegar
were passed around several times
soldiers need meat on their bones
martin
walking through dustbowls
hailstorms
riding on the blade
of a lightning rod
those old sisters
opened
their front rooms for you
opened preserves and jams
that had been put away
for something special
you were a something special
tall, brown, sweet with dreams
like their own sons
when they were about your age
before they drowned
in the dust
that you so gallantly
stepped lightly through—
these were your first infantry, martin,
GRANDMOTHERS

whose words and dreams
shot straight bullets
these were your first line
GRANDMOTHERS
always ready to rinse out
a soul or two
these were the first line who put the armor
of sassafras, high john the conqueror, and
blood root
inside your shoes
made mountains continue to grow
in your daytime dreams.
yes, martin, songs
sung in kitchens
on front porches
in turnip patches
at hog-killings
carried the same verses
carried the same weapons
carried the same vision
in your name they gathered
washing, sharpening knives
polishing bullets
painting numbers
on their children's heads

stolen names

when winds blow strong inside your head
step back outside
greet the morning
touch the blind
whisper into their torn coat pockets
there is pain in the sun's shadow
this morning
there are scorched faces
there are windows that don't close

but come back inside
there's a lap
there's a lover
there's a prayer
when winds blow strong inside your head
step back outside
greet the sun
and know your own name

for jonathan

you who call yourself warrior
you who rename yourself
in the season of combat
the season called preparation
we stand at the portals of your arrival
we bear gifts to your secrecy
to the codes of decency
self-respect confidence
righteousness
you rename yourself
in this season of motherhood
in the arms of southern charm
in the shadow of inequity
in the faces of family
we who hold the wind
sand
rain
fire
of your wintertime

will learn your new name
will celebrate your fullness
will hold back the curtains
and watch you fly
in the morning
of your season
mothers
grandmothers
fathers
grandfathers
aunts uncles cousins
herald your coming
in the time of delicious newness
and increased knowledge
we herald your learning
we celebrate your choice of weapons
your strength
in this season called harvest
we gather in your renaming

come home gordon
beyond the griots
    sacred as psalms
    listen to the wind
    it marks your history

for segun

nighttime
keeper of son moon-cradled tears
mother reaches inside knotted twisted boughs
tears flow upward back into eyes
with birthing shadows
not a time to be born
history repeats itself
grim reaper snatches pacifiers
    of allurement/pacifiers
    of question
you curl beside your own lighthouse
    your own beacon
    your own guiding flash
into a nighttime that keeps you lately.

for donald and segun

125th street market
beggars
choosers
priests unfinished unpainted
voodoo dolls for sale
    the priest sold cowrie shells
    his wife sold necklaces made
    from elephant hair
    they exchanged ivory for words
the city dresses up for mandela
winos reappear in the family album
needles fall from the arms
of alley squirrels
we run to take cover out of the rain

a declaration of peace/
a time of thankful praise

i will bear roots and walk inside you
prepare the morning to meet you
i will know peace but will not know thirst
because of you
i will know beauty but will not know fear
because of you
i will know a world but will not know echoes
because of you
death is a five o'clock door
forever changing time
a morning without sun or shadow
a morning already afternoon
i unrolled bandages of civilized wounds
and danced
chanting rituals inside your
wounds
morning is the same as night
death and life are one

for i have declared peace
with the seasons
the wintertime and springtime
of my womb are the same
both seasons bear marbleized
children
who become ambushed by life
a century of cancer
a century of singing the wrong
songs
dancing the wrong dances
but i have prepared a place for you
i have prepared a song for you to sing
a dance for you to dance
i will restring your eyes for
you
i will restring your body for
you
i will restring peace for you
and may you walk
proud
carrying this new string
of love
at the center of death is birth
for i have declared a day
of peace for your soul
for my soul
you pyramid
my mother
our feet were chained
together in egypt
our voices
marched before the
sunrise

our army scattered the
dead faces
inside cereal bowls
children ask why are the other children always
hungry
why are the other children
always sick
always hurting
always dying
i call back to you this memory
fresh with pain
but it is well for i have
declared this moment a moment
of passing
a moment to receive
i will bear roots
and walk inside you
the buffalo-walk of death
death is coming
to give birth
for i have declared
this a day of singing
we will sing in
the mountains
we will sing in the
earth's night-moments
i shall inhale ancient
black breath
and cry for every
living and every dying
creature
for i have come to the
middle of my circle
and i must pray

i must scream
i must shout
i must survive this
moment called peace
i will know peace but
will not know thirst
because of you
i will know beauty but
will not know fear because of you
i will travel but will
not become the traveler
because of you
i shall declare war
but will not kill
nations because of you
instead you
will swallow my tears
and eat fully from
my breasts
you will learn our
songs
and listen with your
tongues
speak with your eyes
for i have declared peace
and this love will become you
and you will learn to wear it well

...gone fishing

two poles
two men
bearers of family crest
heirloom secrets
baiting southern streams
with iron tears
caribbean
samoan
hawaiian
disillusion
sepia scenes
recreated on augusted nights
another future
another hand holding soil
remake the family tree
put the roots in water
shave the bark
cut the branches
boil the leaves

bearers of new
trees
stripped
secrets
cleansed by
harvest of
tears
swim
upward
outward
recreate
other lights
other soils
drowning
other soils
drowning
who held
back the
roots

drink the buds
sprouting roots
strangling children
two poles
two men
dip into icy
atlantics
plant broad flatness
inside curves

who only
gave
two men
two poles
but no
instructions
to fish

song of alice/ossie/ nathaniel/ivory

i have drunk your bath water
rubbed the liniment of time
into crusting wounds
out of a windowless womb
you all climbed
out of my grandmother
named eva
you crawled
stood looking back up into vulva
up into her soul's crevice
standing on tiptoes holding
onto the womb's lid
you reach back up inside. wait for me.

i have loved all the people
i can love
the walls bleed back
your hands bloody
moist but alive

you slept as i crawled
down this mountain
you slept in her foothills
in her valley
you ate from her hair
waiting for me.

Jaki Shelton Green

Jaki Shelton Green is a community activist and writer. She has worked as an Arts and Education Consultant and as a Community Economic Development Consultant. She is working on a Juke Joint project which is partially funded by the North Carolina Arts Council. She has performed her poetry and taught workshops in the United States, the Caribbean, Europe, and Brazil.

Jaki Shelton Green's poetry has appeared in textbooks, journals, anthologies, and publications such as the *Crucible, The African-American Review, Esssence* magazine and *Obsidian.* Her works include *Dead on Arrival, Dead on Arrival and New Poems, Masks,* and *Blue Opal,* a play. She is a contributing author to *Pete and Shirley: The Great Tar Heel Novel,* and is completing a collection of short stories.

CPSIA information can be obtained
at www.ICGtesting.com
Printed in the USA
JSHW020322050523
41307JS00002B/3